Advance Praise fc

These unflinching poems take us deep into the psycne oi a mother whose daughter has been taken over by addiction. In language that fuses art and emotion with integrity, Greenspan shows us there are no easy answers, that struggle in itself is an act of fierce love. In "The War on Drugs," one of the participants at a gathering of parents of addicts says, "I'm not here for hope I'm here for courage." The Heroin Addict's Mother is infused with courage. We all need to read these poems for their remarkable artistry, their craft, their hard-earned lessons.
Kathleen Aguero, Author of *Daughter Of*

Deep, dangerous, exquisite, elegant, terrifying, these poems take the ground away from under the reader just as it was taken away in the poet-mother's life. Heartbreaking and intense, in places Shakespearean.
Phyllis Chesler, Author of *Women and Madness*

In this courageously truthful collection, with lyricism both haunting and compelling, Miriam Greenspan generously shares her view from the trenches. "…from here there's only / live or die / there is no ordinary sky." Greenspan's narrative unfolds under this strange sky where the landscape changes from a loving childhood home to a filthy needle-strewn apartment, to the streets, crack houses, prison, and to the inevitable repeated cycles of detox and rehab. This book is necessary and timely. The number of drug overdose deaths in the United States has exceeded 70,000 for the past several years. Yet, the epidemic of opioid addiction is greeted by woefully inadequate measures. In these poems we are with the mother who pleads, "Where do the mothers go? / To what rough god do we pray?" She cries out not just for her child, but for all our children.
Julia Morris Paul, Poet Laureate of Manchester, Connecticut,
Author of *Staring Down the Tracks*

These poems are beautifully powerful. As someone who has lived with the heartache of loving someone with active addiction and someone who has found recovery, as well as losing a loved one to overdose, I related to every aspect. Miriam's words capture the essence of what we who are touched by addiction live and breathe. *They remind us we are not alone and that we too can recover.*

Joanne Peterson, Executive Director of Learn to Cope, Inc.

These poems are breathtaking, truly brilliant. Destined to be tremendously helpful to so many people going through similar terrifying, gut-wrenching experience and to help others understand in great depth what that world is like.

Paula J. Caplan, Author of *Don't Blame Mother: Mending the Mother-Daughter Relationship*

Greenspan's brave poems, unafraid of darkness and breathtakingly honest, capture the nuances of grief, anger, and love a mother goes through when her child falls into the river of addiction. As a mother of a son who died of a heroin overdose, I can say that these poems echo the complicated breaks in my own heart. A rich mix of sadness and despair, love and hope, there's not a word that doesn't ring true.

Sheryl St. Germain, Author of *The Small Door of Your Death*

A genuine, gritty, and stirring collection of heartfelt poems reflecting the beauty and the beast of raw emotion emanating from the power and persistence of a mother's undying love for her addicted child. These poems will resonate with so many out in the world suffering from addiction.

John F. Kelly, Professor of Psychiatry in Addiction Medicine, Harvard Medical School, Founder/Director, Recovery Research Institute, Mass General Hospital

In The Heroin Addict's Mother, renowned psychologist Miriam Greenspan gifts us with intensely personal, forceful, and courageous poems that speak not only to mothers of addicted children, but to all of us who have feared and fought for our children to be safe and well.

Harriet Lerner, Author of *The Dance of Anger*

Only a true poet can tell such truths with such power. We are stunned and grateful for Greenspan's unrelenting view. Now we know what we couldn't possibly know otherwise. Bless her gift and courage.

Deena Metzger, Author of *Ruin and Beauty*

The Heroin Addict's Mother

A Memoir in Poetry

Miriam Greenspan

atmosphere press

For the mothers who fight for their children's lives
For our daughters and sons, living and dead

For Anna, my green-eyed girl

Contents

III. LOVE THAT WON'T LET UP

When we read the poem as witness, we are marked by it and become ourselves witnesses...
Carolyn Forché

From An Ordinary Sky

a voice on the phone
        a stranger
            says she's found her
                on the street—
                    I must come
                        at once
                            to save her
                                from herself—
                                    the voice repeats
                                        heroin—
                                            she's shooting
                                                heroin in manhattan
                                                    the explosion
                                                is silent
                                            red fireball, all
                                        that's left
                                    of home
                                from here there's only
                            live or die—
                there is no
ordinary sky

Dismemberment

Surely all art is the result of one's having been in danger, of having gone through an experience all the way to the end, where no one can go any further.
Rainer Maria Rilke

In Her Room

where the carpet stains begin
at the door and end at the window
where the air is stale with smoke
from cigarettes lit years ago
where her art class engraving
of a dragon her photo
of a young boy throwing stones
into a pond hang in silence
where I heard her voice
in muted tones beneath the noise
of the TV where girls giggled
on overnights a floor away
from discovery
where she fell asleep with the phone
on her face where her adolescence
took place—the hidden
beer and the boys—
where after college she returned
to hibernate for winter
and never emerged
for spring
where blood spilled
into the needle pills fell
under the bed where spirits
of the addicted dead feed
on the memory of heroin
where the space is not
converted to a guest room
where no one goes anymore
where the door is closed
the past is frozen

West 63rd St.

Find her naked
in a once white towel
in a Westside hovel.

Her face is gone.
In it's place, an omen
of another daughter.

She hasn't eaten
in two weeks.
Feed her.

Buy her a bagel she gets chatty
wants to tell me why
she's on the needle.

Tell me.
Why?
Tell me.

Cooking in a 4-star restaurant is stressful.
she's been lonely.   her dealer is her
friend.   the addicts are her   *family.*

Face it.
On this street, heroin
is her only mother.

Persephone Goes Down

Dead, but not dead.

Gone the dazzling
smile of summer, the clear
green eye, the humor.

Your body's force
divorced from
your body. You're cold
as a corpse. A sweaty
granite statue.

Daughter, you've eaten
the black seeds
of the poppy, trapped
yourself in Hades. Death grows
in you like a baby.

Shall I bury you?

To what gods
shall I pray?
What spirits return
wandering souls?
What angels descend
so far down?

Jumpstart

my heart is dead i hear myself say
leaning my tired arms on the stove
(my back is toward her the only way
i can speak to my mother)
it ran like a racehorse on a 12-day
binge in manhattan it beat
fast and hard on a dark street
in new haven a knife at my throat so close
i could hear the angel's quiver
maybe it burnt itself up   maybe i'm just not
cut out for this world   the first time I shot
smack I was a sunflower
in god's garden   now I can't jumpstart
my dead heart   without the brown powder

she's already gone

leaving skid marks
as she peels off
in her dealer's
wild red Camry
her bill pre-paid
with blow jobs
delivered in the alley
come to think
of it, she must have been
long gone
before
she first extended
her pale arm

I sit like Penelope
knitting a rich blue quilt
to wrap her smashed-
up flesh, soothe
her deadly itch—
the thread of
which unravels
every night, no matter
how tight the stitch

Keep Your Heart Open

when she tells you she's clean
and you find
fresh needles on her bed
keep your heart open
when she nods out
at the table and falls
asleep in her soup
keep your heart open
when her eyes lose their fire
her face a pallid
cunning mask
keep your heart open
when she speaks baby talk
to the dog then locks herself
into the bathroom
to shoot up
keep your heart open
when she takes out a knife
to clean her fingernails
keep your heart open
when she stands at the window
and you don't
let her in
keep your heart open
when you imagine her
on a dark street at midnight
walking into her
last crackhouse
keep your heart open
when sirens wail
you think it's her
in the ambulance the police car
keep your heart open
when you convince the court
to lock her up so she won't
kill herself with smack
crack and benzos
keep your heart open
when her eyes grow wide
with venom

12

keep your heart open
when you sit facing her
in an orange plastic chair
in Framingham Prison
keep your heart open
when she gets out
and falls back down
the hole that has no bottom
keep your heart open
to her iron resolve
to keep up the lie
keep your heart open
when the black sky
parts and a thin beam
of light breaks through
reminding you
of who she was once
keep your heart open
when the sky closes
again   again   again
keep your heart open
when you have no heart
left to open

Detox #1

The month she detoxed
at McLean, Lindsay Lohan
did the same in California
Britney Spears bizarrely
sheared her hair and had her kids
abruptly taken from her
Amy Winehouse not yet dead
wailed *no no no I won't go go go*
Rehab was celebrity chic
a rite of passage for attractive
gifted young addicted females—
my girl had found her niche.
Binge drinking just another day
on campus oxycontin cool
in high school xanax vicodin
readily available right off
the bathroom shelf. Heroin
soon to be declared an epidemic
white educated twenty-somethings
the new smack demographic.
She was lucky they had a bed
in a clean well-lit place
where she could get
suboxone the replacement
opiate newly designed to stave off
the craving. On Proctor I, it was enhanced
by ativan to make withdrawal
painless. Dispensed by a perky nurse
in a whitewashed hallway
at a Harvard hospital with a very nice
brochure, we were hopeful—
until we overheard a patient say
spin-dry referring to repeated
detox cycles beloved by young addicts
who come in to dry out
before another run.
When she put her dirty clothes
and toothbrush in a cubby
in the room she shared with a 40-year-old
crumpled addict on a fresh-made bed

my only reference point was
the first day of camp
or college. Only this time
when I left her she wasn't smiling
she was crying *Mommy!*
How did I get here?

People Mean Well

They say cut her off
   Don't let her in
They say hold her close
   Don't let her go
They say it's not her fault
   It's an illness
They say it's not your fault
   You're good parents
They say don't let her do this
   You're enabling
They say it's a phase
   She'll outgrow it
They say it could be worse
   She's not dead yet

Let's Talk About Addiction

Let's talk about addiction
the CIA connection, drug money
to finance covert shipments
of weapons, hidden wars,
that baby lying dead
on the streets of Kabul
and your daughter in her quilted bed
with a blackened spoon and syringe.

Let's talk about Mr. Gagliardi
of Medford who died at midday
on the grass in Boston Garden
shooting up in front of tourists
who found a fresh corpse
where they expected red and yellow tulips.
Crowds on their way
to catch a play on Washington Street
were treated to front row seats
of theatre verité, the last act
in which the needle hangs
from the dead man's arm
while the faint of heart turn away.

Let's talk about suicide,
direct and inadvertent. Vehicular homicide,
that last joyride before the lifelong spin
in the wheelchair. Let's talk about theft,
crimes committed as a means
to get high. Let's not forget
random acts of violence
in which heroin meth crack
cocaine drive the live action
thriller in the killer's brain.

Let's talk about the purity of high-octane
smack, unmixed, for the cost
of a six-pack, grown for your loved ones
in rich Afghan fields of poppy
by farmers with nothing else to sell
but their daughters.

Let's talk about your teenage son
who thought snorting oxycontin
would be fun and wound up
strung out, breaking into homes
for trinkets. Look past the picket fences
you'll find the lawn disturbed
in your neighbor's yard. Note the crimson
cardinal and his red-crested mate.
To face the Hydra-headed god
who's kidnapped your child, you'll need
a bracing shot of beauty the way
an end-stage drunk needs booze.

The War On Drugs

Niobe, your tears/are your children now. See how/we have multiplied.
Hayden Carruth

Sitting at the weekly meeting of parents, the mother—
her lined face a stark map of the common road
we travel—says what we all know: *we are soldiers
on the front lines of a war for our children's souls.*

She's come from California to keep company
with her heroin-using daughter, in a one room flat
in Boston, trying—as every one of us has tried—
to save her child's life.

Under different circumstances she'd be writing
Hollywood screenplays, but today
she's asking whether the comfort she provides—
brushing her girl's long tresses, holding her

bony body in the dark—
only makes it more comfortable for her to use.
*Do what you need to do
for you* says the 12-step devotee.

The business class mother in the corner
can't stop asking *Why
am I here and not on vacation in Tuscany?*
The corduroy guy in the swivel chair replies

*Don't envy the civilians. Say good-bye
to normal. Try to keep your balance
on the tattered high-wire.*
The man in suit and tie says

These meetings are a joke—they offer him no hope.
The mother of two sons in jail for dope—
the one with eyes like Hiroshima—cries
I'm not here for hope I'm here for courage.

Battalion Of Two

Dearest, we are two soldiers
in a common trench
we feed each other cracked
crackers and tins of sardines
pour water down each other's throats
from rusty old canteens
our sleep is short
with interruptive dreams

lying in wait
for the next round of fire
we take a minute to amuse
ourselves with music
words and schemes

the enemy is invisible
strange and intimate
as our children's severed
feet and hobbled brains

medics of every stripe traipse
through at dawn waving
stethoscopes crying *Carry On!*

limbs fly   on clouds
livers impale   on blades
the air buckles   and seethes

each day we dip our heads
into the earth seeking refuge
from the air   at night
we sleep upright leaning
on each other's backs

When She Heard Her Sister
Was A Drug Addict

The first thing she said *Can this kill you?*
got straight to the heart of the matter.

When her sister said yes, she cried
I'm scared you'll die.

Again, the heart. Then
have you gone to a meeting?

Which she gleaned from watching
Stuart Smalley Saves His Family

Five times. And the punchline:
you need help!

Obvious to everyone but her sister.
Last: *I love you. I want you to be safe.*

They say she's slow, but she was
quicker than any of us.

What Grandma Knew

1.
I swore as a child I'd always protect her.
She didn't have to know I was nearly raped
in the Bahamas on spring break. Or that I smoked.

There was no way to conceal the baby's death.

She walked out of her house in Queens
and roamed the streets. This housewife who could deliver
an impromptu lecture on the history of the Jews
from the fall of the Second Temple right through
to the present—with a special first-person focus
on the European period just before my birth—
the river of blood running from Poland
to my south Bronx childhood—
This woman who could speak
Yiddish, Polish, English, Russian, and recite
by heart the poetry of Alexander Pushkin,

fell dark and silent as a shroud.

All her memory erased at once.
She wandered up and down Queens Boulevard
until a neighbor found her, reduced
to a single question

Dead? Aaron is dead?

She kept asking, as if
her grandson—air-lifted into the next
world after a two-month visit—might return
if she asked again.

2.
My mother and sleep were never friends.
Before dawn, the memories would rise, of life before
the house of Europe's Jews incinerated—
leaving only her, the youngest, to remember
each member of her family.

Her father, Zvi, the only one who died
of natural causes—the typhus they both caught
when she was three, and only she returned
from the hospital. Her mother, Miriam, the devout
young widow who relied completely on her five children,
whose last trip with her two older daughters was to Czestochowa,
in vain and desperate hope that Hitler might refrain
from taking Jews protected by the Black Madonna.
Mostly she recalled her oldest brother Jacob
who accompanied his six-year old son from the bunker
to the *Umschlagplatz*, where the Nazis assisted them on board
to Auschwitz. The second brother, Sam, the looker,
family joker, spent too much time chasing pigeons,
starved to death in the Lodz ghetto, saving himself
from the gas chamber. The middle sister, Bella,
who embroidered golden birds and roses,
with whom she stayed up late, speaking heatedly
of books and socialist utopia. And Anna,
the solemn eldest sister, who had a child before
they took her to Treblinka.
Perhaps she saw the little girl at play
dressed in white, a bright
red ribbon in her long black hair.

3.
Mama, now you're ninety-five, and I must break
My vow, find a way to say

Your gifted grandchild, named for your exterminated sister,
Shoots a deadly drug into her veins.

But it's you who breaks our unspoken pact
In the bright downstairs apartment where you've lived for years

The spartan life of the Survivor.
I don't want to tell you. I want to spare your tears.

*But you have to know. She burst into my bedroom
In the middle of the night. What could she be looking for?*

Your jewels, Mama. Your cash. Her fix.
We sat together on your bed,

Covered by the gold threadbare bedspread of my childhood,
Holding each other's hands and weeping.

Breaking a lifetime of agnostic doubt, you prayed
God help her! Please God, help her!

In the matter-of-fact manner you've perfected, you said
I've lived too long.

Just For Today

Just for Today don't forget to breathe
while choking. Stop dreaming
your escape. When all you can think is
when the call will come
Just for Today means
Present Moment Only Moment
and all that Buddhist jazz
that doesn't pertain much
when you're watching your child shoot up
Just for Today don't strap yourself to the underside
of a car and ride it out. Don't run away
(not a problem in my case, I'd rather stay
till they bring in the dogs to sniff out the dead body)
Just for Today is a reminder not to be a martyr
be kind to yourself, do something
that feels good, which is counter-intuitive
when you're schooled in altruistic motherhood
Just for Today eat a bagel and cheese
while she nods out on the couch
Just for Today take a walk in the park
while she goes prowling in the dark recesses of the city
Just for Today immerse yourself in a bath
to wash off her last withdrawal rant, rub your body
with unguents and, to preserve your sanity, imagine
you're the Queen of Sheba
Just for Today means you're not alone
if you remember the companionship of fellow travellers
on the cratered road to *godknowswhere*
Just for Today go to a meeting when you're strung out
about your family member's friendly visitor program
by which she welcomes homeless addicts
into her house, and one of them
rapes her. Go to a meeting, they say,
until you like going. Never mind that you're not
the gregarious sort, you'd rather resort to writing
an interior monologue than tell your war story
to a room packed with veterans. Go
even if you're not a team player, not a joiner,
oppositionally-defiant, temperamentally a loner

25

Go because there's nothing
else to do, even your prayers are empty
Just for Today forgive yourself
if you can't taste a thing that's not bitter

The Heroin Addict's Mother

I imagine a guillotine—
The sharp blade, the jeering crowd—

What shall I do with my head,
Now that it's lopped off?

Carry it on a stake,
With its high blush of shame?

Hide it in the basement,
Hoping no one goes down?

Somewhere or other there's glamour
In serving lines of cocaine.

But not   no never   ever—
A needle   a tie   and a spoon.

After the kids are locked up
For the crime of getting high

After the littered hallways
After the *junkies* are trashed,

Where do the mothers go?
To what rough god do we pray?

Who brings us casseroles?

The New Face Of Heroin

is not cash-poor,
easy to ignore, black
urban underclass

she's young, white
private-schooled,
privileged and pretty

living with her parents
in a single-family colonial
outside of the city

the new face of heroin
captures your eye
with L'Oreal, not Maybelline

she can pay the cost
of Percoset and Vicodin
until the money's short

when the pills
run out, heroin
steps in

the new face of heroin
calls a well-worn number
on her cell-phone

when she's jittery,
drives a Honda Civic to the store,
prefers home delivery

Standard Advice From Experts

Don't offer her shelter or money even if
   She's hungry. Don't give her a thing
She hasn't earned. Let her suffer

The consequences of her actions. Teach her,
   Through operant conditioning, that if she spends
All her dough on dope, she'll end up homeless.

How can she learn consequences if
   The only thing that matters is her next fix? I want to ask
But think better of it. And why will no one speak of
                                           Death

As a probable consequence of her actions?
   They tell me I'm the quintessential
Model of a born enabler.

They say: see to your own disease. Practice not losing
   Your temper. Keep the lines of communication
Open—even if she's using.

I imagine myself breathing
   Deeply while my daughter, eyes pinned,
Locks herself into her room, screaming

Cunt bitch! Leave me the fuck alone!
   I imagine myself speaking in even tones,
Without a hint of emotion—

Honey, do you really need that next fix?
   How about a bowl of Mint Chocolate Chip?
I imagine myself pleading

Baby, your brain's lit up with smack, so maybe
   You might re-consider treatment? And if you won't go,
My sweet, allow me to show you the street.

Exile

We all carry within us our places of exile, our crimes, and our ravages
Albert Camus

1.
No civilian can know what they know,
What they would say—
If they could speak of it—
Returning from wars far away

To patriotic chants that omit
The exile
Of trying to forget
What cannot be forgotten.

2.
Others, not soldiers, who left places like Santiago,
Recalling home—
The wide avenues, the overpowering scent of orchids, the
uniformed men
On the street corners—spend their lives
Trying to remember.

3.
Long sequestered in hopelessness,
The human heart exiles itself—
An expulsion made more complete
By being chosen.

Some sit on the sidewalks in battered disarray,
Veins popping in a vise of homemade elastic ties,
They tap the powder in the spoon, heat it—shoot it—
Not knowing if they live or die.

Families of the drug-afflicted—living alongside the needle—
Are banished to their shrouded cave
Of pain, far from the plain world of everyday—
The world lost, lost as a child is lost

Who one moment stands on the shore,
The next, is swept away.

Digging His Son's Grave

PBS chronicles the epidemic. Easy heroin, cheap death.
We watch together, mother and daughter

In our separate worlds of pain. On the screen
The pale father points to the grave

He's dug in his yard. The blank stone
Awaits his son's name.

It comforts him that his son would come home
At last. Not die on the street, alone.

Rehearsing for the day, he remembers
Who his son was, before the drug took him. Dead,

His boy would find a modicum of peace
And he, a cruel respite from the dread.

Gratitude

You sleep in your childhood bed
   Hugging your paraphernalia like a lover.
Last night I saw the blue flower

At your inner elbow.
   What's that? I asked
As if I didn't know.

I bumped my arm! Get out!
   You raged, and for extra measure
Threw a broken lamp down the corridor.

This morning I beseech the spirits. I remember
   You are one of the children of God
Even with your darkened eyes matted hair

And—rising from your body—
   The sour smell of despair.
This morning on the porch

I sit and watch the sparrow
   Watching me, and feel in every cell
The small bird's song.

Dismemberment

The medicine woman does nothing
  herself, only opens to the spirits
  and does their bidding

In service to the sick.
  Panther and Hawk, Wolf and Tree
  arrive when she calls them.

They protect and guide her
  as she journeys into worlds
  no one else will visit.

Sometimes they turn
  on her. Hawk punctures
  her flesh, blood gushing

From the holes. Wolf attacks
  her throat, splitting body
  from head. Panther tears

Her limbs, leaving her
  in pieces.
  Tree sits and sees.

Unless the shaman willingly submits
  to their cruel beneficence,
  even the spirits are helpless.

Knack For Survival

The important thing...is not to be cured, but to live with one's ailments.
Albert Camus

mother of the addict recovers speech

street girl burnt shirt
gray face blue tracks

gone girl green eyes
gone gone gone gone

re-hab short stay
run a-way in a storm

smack calls
hope gone

girl home save life
again hope feel safe

locked room blood wall
call police no use

motherheart too soft
tough up throw out

on street live die
motherheart cut out

each day death near
let go how? *how?*

don't know
don't know

don't stop
don't give up
don't give up
don't stop
don't
give up

come home try again
new start same end

Stigma/Stigmata

she wore her stigmata the way they all did her tribe held in the talons of the god who lifted and gripped them and filled them with the power of ingested percoset parachuted oxycontin snorted dilaudid crushed vicodin the power that grew in them when they became expert pill poppers in middle school and graduated to cooking heroin shooting up in high school bathrooms between algebra and gym   she bore her stigmata like the pistil in a flowering plant receiving the pollen like the goddess opening to welcome the holy insemination   like a crucifixion   bleeding from the tracks the world nailed into the despised disgraced displaced disowned consoled only by the one true merciful living god heroin she knew her god was a dissembler   she cursed him even as he delivered her   she knew one day he would kill her   there's a back door to the left-behind world so they told her but the door is so far and so small it is easier for a camel to go through the eye of a needle than for a *junkie* to return to the world   to find the door she'd have to renounce running buying selling tricking shooting chasing the high that would fix the sickness she'd have to break through the Stigma she couldn't see it she couldn't imagine it before she'd crawl toward some distant door that didn't exist she'd head straight for what she knew best she'd get the one thing that worked   she'd willingly bleed from all the stigmata to open her skin to the god

The (Un)Dead

The Heroin Road in the Underneath
Is paved with bodies of the dead.

Severed opiated heads, like poisoned planets,
Spin in fetid air. Pinned pupils stare, deadly.

Some survive the white plague's scythe
As nomads in the alleys

Invisible in plain sight—hungry ghosts
With dirty hair dirty eyes dirty lies

Smacked-out outlaws
Stuck like slugs on the sidewalk.

They too had mothers once
Who combed their shiny, shampooed hair

Cooed like doves into scrubbed, pink ears.
She is one—my pomegranate daughter

Who slumps and nods and mumbles
While all around her, fires smolder

Ashes fall and crumble.

Knack For Survival

you have a knack
for survival
like your grandparents
who outlived Hitler
but your wounds
are self-inflicted
the wiry cuts
crossing your wrists
the blue tracks
lining your arms
the red scabs
dotting your body
from where you picked
the skin off—
like pulling ticks
from a dog—
but no marks
so spectacular
as the burns
you engraved the day
you doused yourself
with lighter fluid
threatening to set
yourself on fire
if I didn't give you
cash for smack—
then struck the match
and lit up
like a greasy barbecue grill
and I smothered
the blue flames
rising from your belly
with a beige sofa pillow
saving your raw
animal hide but not
your blackened soul

Cause & Effect

because where there is damage
there must have been that first nick
in the stocking before
it came undone a chain reaction
of domino effects a cascade
of tumbling objects a single atom
multiplied an amoeba split
through binary fission

because amidst the litter on the pinewood floor the bloody
burn holes in the mattress the needles used and unused

because there are a host of biologic certainties that explain
how bodies work in an orderly fashion because since the
dawn of time humans have seen design
in the cosmos because the unified field of consciousness the
seven interconnected seas
the Big Bang the expanding universe giant clouds of
primordial elements coalescing
to form stars and galaxies

because amidst the litter on the pinewood floor the bloody
burn holes in the mattress the needles used and unused

because nature abhors a vacuum because
there can be nothing
without something nor can there be
something without nothing because
there is nothing
so whole as a broken heart
because there is nothing so broken
as a mind bereft of reason
because of the cycles of the trees and of the seasons

because amidst the litter on the pinewood floor the bloody
burn holes in the mattress the needles used and unused

because the mystery of good and evil
is filled to brimming with potential

41

explanations because the mind at sea clings tightly
to its life-raft because the ego insists
there must be some principle that holds it all together
because chaos isn't comforting
because mystery is insufficient at 4:48 in the morning

because amidst the litter on the pinewood floor the bloody
burn holes in the mattress the needles used and unused

If Only

if you could have run off into a field, into the woods
if you could have run from your sister's broken
legs, arms, clavicle, wrist—
away from the nebulizer stoking its medicinal mist
into her lungs. If I'd been with you cheering
when you first rode your pink two-wheeler
down the street, not glued to a seat
in the emergency room
if you hadn't seen your sister's crooked back stiffen
with the seizures, the white spittle foaming
from the small frozen mouth
if you could have stopped her
from falling, if you'd walked out
of the pre-op waiting room before
the surgeons sharpened their utensils
if you'd gone to a secret place
to rage in—a tree house, a cave—
if you'd flown out of the narrow cage
of our chaos into the arms of someone
not encumbered by the daily noise
of your sister's pain
if you'd found a place that stayed
the same, that never changed
a flat and grassy plain, not
the iron mountain we climbed daily—

would you never then have run
into the beer, the vodka, rum,
that first exquisite
needle?

After

1.
after he threw her against
the fence, pulled her down

in the dark, ripped
her pants off, raped her

after the knife at her neck
the condom on his prick

to erase any trace
of his sickness

after she took two days
to tell me, so she could weigh

the threats he made
against her, after the ER

hook-up, after she tore
out her leads

after the doctor refused
to give klonopin

to a *junkie*
after the panting ER panic

after the ranting
after the two cops stopped

asking questions, after the detective
closed the door behind him

after the ripping of a fabric,
once whole, now composed

of dangling threads—
came the last unraveling—

till not even a strand was left

2.
there are needles in a box amidst the litter
but they look old. more likely, it's the cocktail
of downers she takes to induce a stupor
that approximates that first never-to-be-repeated
perfect high. half naked on the couch,
she's talking in her sleep—
the Spanish guy takes less here's two hundred.
I'm here to wake her up and take her
to the ER the second time this week.
I plead and yell, cajole. I play loud
rock & roll. her father rouses her at last
with a cold bottle of ice blue Gatorade
against her skin. watch her slide in a pool of urine
gleaming like floor polish on the hardwood
floor of her apartment clotted debris
of nights of drug use mixed with dog pee
along the corridor from back to front—
product of the black and white pitbull
belonging to the homeless couple
crashing in her place. they ran out so fast
the orange tabby cat escaped.

3.
her brain that, at age two
knew the Latin names of fish
from the glossy book
we read together in the tub
now recites in gibberish
half-remembered drug deals
skin like alabaster, wrecked
with tracks and evidence
of forced entry
a soul at once familiar
and unrecognizable
as in a horror movie
where the innocent girl's mouth
opens, and out come
snakes and vipers
I've seen it all—

the grime
on the floor table bed
the dirt on every
surface, the garbage
in every nook
each night I see you
skinned and hanging
from a jagged hook

The Hearts Of The Mothers

We are sweeping the world's debris
With our small brooms and pails.

We are cleansing the waterfalls, so the waters flow
Like buttermilk for morning pancakes.

We are singing songs for the dreamers.
We are cooking soup from scraps.

We are holding pans for the old ones.
Our children dance on our bones.

We offer long breasts to the feeders.
Watch them stride, satiated, into the wide world.

What we say into the ears of the dying
Speeds them on their way.

We wash the blood from their bodies.
Our fingers close their eyes.

We are not martyrs. We are not monsters.
We are not saints. We are not arbiters of worldly matters.

We are not the wide-legged ones who ride
Fire-breathing horses across the plains of the earth.

We are the silent ones.
With our own hands, we cover our mouths.

If heard, the hearts of the mothers would crack
Open the world.

Rehab #2

In the first group therapy session
of her second rehab in Florida, when they tried
to coax her into facing her traumatic childhood
with her disabled sister, she wasn't having any of it.

She was adamant that her memory
of a happy childhood was accurate
and that, unlike the two women in group
who'd been sexually abused, she wasn't in denial.

She remembered sharing the same bedroom,
the bunk bed ritual where she whispered *tickle tickle*
and her sister giggled *where's the pickle?*
How they laughed each night before they said *sleep tight.*

Twenty-eight days later, fed up
with her never-ending non-compliance,
even after they put her on the highest dose
of Seroquel recommended by science,

They sent her packing
to the halfway house where,
despite the daily urines, buying smack
was easier than ever.

Relapse # 3

Again, the dread. Something's dead. A carcass
In the cracked cage of my heart.

Again the caving in. Ashen skin
Vacant eyes. The foul shovel of her lies

Digging her deeper, deeper in-
To the familiar rank decay.

Again her room disheveled—a plume
Of disarray. Bloodstains

On her shirt again, the same
Size as the cigarette burns.

Heavy-lidded zombie nodding
On my couch, sneaking around my house,

Stealing my days.
Again my brain in high gear. Arms raised

To fight, feet set to flee, heart pumping to act.
Then, the sudden drop

Of pulse. Action without aim.
Motion without force.

Again. Again the dire game
Of wait-and-see.

Survive or die.
This time, which will it be?

One Day At A Time

after everything else has been tried and failed, I drop her
at the homeless shelter, where—

(First Things First)

right off, she's greeted by the Hollywood picture
of a small-time dealer—

(Keep Coming Back)

backwards sports cap and bling, black and blue
tattoos covering his arms and neck—

(Live and Let Live)

I swerve the car, hard, to get away, fast and far
from Pine Street Inn—

(Easy Does It)

oxymoronic on this pockmarked street
in the stinking heat in the bowels of Boston—

(Turn It Over)

being a tough-love mother,
they say, is a way to recover—

(Keep It Simple)

but leaving her here with her dealer
I'm the procurer, handing my girl to a slaver

A Good Day

Today my grief is walled off like a cyst
  Enclosed in its dark sac.
No seepage in surrounding cells.

I forget I ever saw a blackened spoon.
  The living and the dead
This moment leave no trace.

Ancient sedimentary ruminations
  Settle in an oceanic trench.
Only you and me, sky-gazing

Through the urban trees,
  Whispering in code, silly old
Married couple conspiracies.

Ghost In The Machine

1.

Forged checks, stolen credit cards, gold jewelry, the cash
she tried to lift from grandma's dresser
in the dead of night—She took anything in sight
but drew a line at stealing her sister's disability check.

She held it in her hand the day I stared her down.
Ordinarily, she'd be spoiling for a fight
but this time, she looks right at me and I can see
a small mote of herself in her eye
as she thrusts her arm forward
and mashes the check into my palm. Even high,
she can still decide to suck some dealer's dick
before she rips off her crippled sister.

This matters, doesn't it? Wild with craving, crazy
as the worst hopped-up addict in withdrawal,
there must still be some capacity to choose—
without which not a single addict would recover.

That same night, I fight with my husband.
He says *It's time to throw her off the bus*
before we crash.
I say *Over my dead body.*

Other nights we reverse positions, argue till we're raw
as burnt flesh. The questions inextinguishable
fires burning minds too numb to think.

Can this really be the same glad-handed girl
who spoke to frogs and salamanders?
Is this our daughter or the drug
making its own decisions?

When you zombie in, eyes pinned,
gauging the proximity of my handbag,
I don't know what to think.

2.
The easy armchair pundit can sit in easy judgment

52

of the likes of Philip Seymour Hoffman. Dispense with the
    lot—
addicts with their grimy moral lapses.
Pontificate on the characterological failures that predate
the inevitable slide down to the needle.

At the other side of the either/or divide in this persistent
cultural debate, the medical expert claims addiction is a
    biochemical disease,
pure and simple. Like diabetes. The brain's craving for
    oblivion
like HIV or blocked arteries. Theft, lies, cruelty, deceit—
just symptoms.

Can there be acts without an actor
forced by the poisoned brain's
impossible-to-resist compulsion? Actions taken
words spoken by a non-existent person—
a non-self, with no memory of self—

—a ghost in the machine?

I prefer the shaman's explanation—
        a chunk of her soul   broken off
            through trauma and sorrow
            the drug   a demon   that takes hold
in the vacuum.

O precious soul! Where's the magician
    who'll bring me back my girl?

    3.
What kind of love is this that refuses
to stop—singing on top of the grave
dug in preparation for her final run?
Is this the unconditional
love the sages speak of?
or a sorry remnant
of maternal instinct, an effulgence
of the heart that, like a rupturing
appendix, is vestigial?
To love an active addict

the rules of relationship must be
suspended. They hang
in air, a bridge to nowhere—
love of someone insubstantial
as a vapor—love feeding on memory,
nothing to grab hold of
but the unforeseen
possibility—each day I see you—
long blonde hair braided
down your back, ruddy complexion
to counter the ashen mask
that you've become.
I see you as you used to be/
or truly are/   or could be/   if only

The Hard Luck Club

My friend says Mr. Right
Turned overnight to Mr. Wrong
The moment the words *endometrial cancer*
Were pronounced. The next day he was gone.

This reminds me of the time my son was born,
His brain done in by intrauterine anoxia—
My bosom friend took one look and ran.
Then again the disaster
Of disability in another child
Made two more friends run even faster.

These quick pivotings are familiar
To those who suffer cancer
Or divorce, or fall, suddenly,
With great force, down the corporate ladder
To the unemployment line.

If your son jumps off the Tobin Bridge
Into the open water, expect one less dinner guest.
Please forgive the parents' panic
When your child graduates from college
To the street. Who can blame them
If they want to keep their distance
From the open maw of fate?

No one wants to be swallowed up
And spit out by bad fortune
Or, through contagion, catch the accident
That hit that lovely girl looking out her window
At the bright, lost world.

No one wants to be a member
of the Hard Luck Club,
Where you sit at the table by invitation only,
And pay your karmic debt
With all the other members
Who know well—

Sometimes the worse it gets, the worse it gets.

No Bottom

Remember the time you smashed the cellar window
  and broke in, after riding around in your used Toyota
    with your brown powder and spoon?

You needed shelter from the street. We needed shelter
  from you. Wily addict, you found a way, bypassed the door
    and slept, curled up, on the concrete floor.

Three nights later we packed you up,
  the cops escorted you out—dragging your bag of stains
    into the freezing rain.

From the porch I watched you limp
  down the lamplit street.
        We keened like old Greek women at a wake.

Sargent McGonagle was sympathetic
  You're doing the right thing. You're helpless
  'till she hits bottom.

You never did hit. Like a shade in Gehenna,
  you float from one dark whim to another—
    with or without the powder.

Broken Cord

There's no explaining what you've done
or why. Lie by lie,
you cut the tender cord
connecting you and I. Corrupted
Medusa, you've turned to stone
the gaze of love that once
flowed from my eyes.
When you approach, I hide
my valuables. Words freeze
in my mouth. I hold myself apart,
unplug my heart
like an obsolete machine.

And Still

The night of dread
  is upon me
And still relentless love
  beats on for the ruined
And still the pink dawn
  beckons at the sill
And still the gold dog
  licks my outstretched hand
And still my wild man
  brews me jasmine tea
And still the sun
  pours in like melting butter
And still these words
  spurt up like a spring

Since You Asked

What's it like to be the mother of a junkie?

Do you really want to know? Are you willing to go down
the hole that has no bottom?

Then imagine: your daughter's been abducted
to an unknown country, where her seductive captor

Holds a pistol to her head, and plays with her
a non-stop game of *Russian Roulette.*

From time to time she sends you snapshots
of a girl who's not your own—

A shell—with a brain so *blankened*
she's forgotten her own name and where she came from.

You call in the very best detectives and tell them
she has *Stockholm Syndrome.* But she doesn't show up

In any of their networks. And though you never stop
searching streets and stars for signs and portents,

You cover all the mirrors in your house with black cloth—
like a Jew in mourning.

There's no calendar to mark the passage of this grief
or tell you when to take the covers off

To see your face—which has turned into the face of someone
    else.
For all practical purposes,

She's dead. Yet she shows up now and then,
and you celebrate by tearing all the covers from the mirrors—
    and that very night, again

She disappears. And so it goes, for years, before you get it—
your life will not begin again *if* or *when—*

This, as it is, *is*
your life. And you must live it

With the Mourner's *Kaddish* in your ears.
In your shared nightmare,

She's lost. The car's out of gas.
The train's derailed. The plane's gone down.

There's no way to bring her home.
So you wait and pray

And set out bowls of breadcrumbs
on the window-seat—

All that's left in your empty pantry—
hoping she'll get hungry

For something more nourishing than the black seeds—
And she'll come home, and eat.

Hope

Hope does me no good.
It bubbles from a poisoned spring

Feeding black dreams
Of what might have been

Or could be,
If only.

Better to sit on the hard rock
Of now. Fear not

The succubus—
That demon tentacled to your foot

Is only temporary.
See how the dragonfly

Lifts up
In sapphire flight—

An iridescent luminescence
Dissolving in thin air

The End Of Desire

Desire itself is movement/Not in itself desirable;
Love is itself unmoving,/Only the cause and end of movement
T.S. Eliot

You will do what you do.
I will want what I want.

Why continue the feud?
I want to free you

Of my desire. I want
To say I'm done. I'm done

Trying to find you. I want
My heart to stop quaking.

I want it to break
Beyond mending.

Let's pretend
We don't belong

To each other. I am not
Your mother.

You are not my cherished
Wasted daughter.

The horizon draws near.
I can see beyond.

It's not too far.
It won't be long.

Hawk

From the oak's low limb you peer at me
   Your breast a speckled nest—then suddenly—a quick red
flash
      On brown serrated wings!

Hawk, what do you see?

Show me the higher view—
   How the land flattens, and even the mountains
      Look up!

Let Her Die

I plead: *What must I do*
            to save this child?

The answer comes quick and sure:
            Let her die.

I take it you're being metaphorical
            I say to the gathering silence.

Then it occurs to me:
            Death might be kinder

To her than life.
            No never! I cry to the spirits.

I will do what you wish—
            But not this.

Love That Won't Let Up

But love has pitched its mansion in
The place of excrement;
For nothing can be sole or whole
That has not been rent
                    William Butler Yeats

Motherheart

Tara Destroyer of Demons
Who tramples hell beings and hungry ghosts,
I pray that you save my daughter

Ears she has but cannot hear, eyes
But cannot see. She knows not
Who she is. She belongs to Nothing

Om Tare Tuttare Ture Soha

Tara Mother of Compassion
I give you my heart, pierced
With a mother's longing
For her daughter's well-being

I give you the charred remains
Of motherhood's remembered bliss
I give you my motherheart, mangled
By helplessness

Om Tare Tuttare Ture Soha

Tara Protector of all the Worlds
Take my uprooted instinct to protect
A child who drowns refusing
The offered hand

Om Tare Tuttare Ture Soha

Tara Great Mother
Receive this heart, ripped
From its moorings, that it may be of use

To all the mothers watching over
Sons and daughters lost
In fearful, trackless wildernesses

Om Tare Tuttare Ture Soha

That Which Is Hidden Shall Be Revealed

Old crazy heart—beating too fast
for too long—you can't keep this up
indefinitely. Trusty old friend—
you'll need a shot of digitalis
before nightfall, something
to slow you down. Here comes
the nurse with the terrible temper,
the bedside manner of the Marquis de Sade.
Under the nasty facade—you'd never know it—
she's really not so bad. When she bends down
to administer your medicine, her black hair falls
like a velvet curtain, hiding her kindness,
her enigmatic smile

Black Door

In a murderous time/the heart breaks and breaks/and lives by breaking.
It is necessary to go/through the dark and deeper dark/and not to turn.
Stanley Kunitz

To gaze too long at the abyss
forces you to see
beyond your capacity
which brings you
to your knees. The dark
earth cracks and a vast
Void like a black door
opens. There is no light
so bright as that which shines
from the darkness—
But first you must be
ready to be buried
alive, choking for air,
clawing without
a way out.
Your bones must be
picked clean, leaving
only small white
chips and fragments.
Then the door
becomes a port
of entry. Don't expect to breathe
normally. This is not
a tunnel to life
everlasting. This is the dark
womb in which new life forms.

Another Earth

and then
the things that pleased me
in the past—the touch
of my husband's hand
a flock of geese
rising all at once
across the pond—
register again
alongside the steady keening
in my inner ear

and then
I practice
every day the art
of looking closely
I see
how a hollow log
in a dark wood
can be home to a snail
haven for a squirrel
a dead tree can be
a nesting habitat
for a hawk or bat

and then
at sunset on a silver lake
I hear
with perfect clarity
the aching wail of the common
spotted loon

and then
I feel again
the beauty—eerie,
yet familiar—
and I know that I've survived—
but on another earth
cold and dry and
cratered as the moon

Methadone Mile

The line forms at the right while the stink of putrefaction
from the fish factory next door, wafts up
in the heat of early morning on Topeka Street.
The thirsty keep arriving—
shuffling or rushing, banging on the door
if they're a minute late. The conversation
resounds with *fuck that shit* and *what the fuck.*

This is the church of last resort
where the anointed receive their cup
of biosimilar replacement to stave off
the demonic beast who's sunk its claws
into their brains. The clinic tells the addicts
there's no way to be completely free
of this disease. You will always be a *junkie*
about to happen—in remission, yes, at best
a functional citizen—but sick nonetheless—
like a diabetic.

I've driven my daughter here
each year, prayed in the car as despair
walks in the door to get his fix.
From where I sit it's hard to tell the difference
between the treatment and the sickness.

Still, I've concluded nothing
will stop her from using until
the vacuum of her opiate receptors
is neatly plugged with legal substitution
for the deadly heaven of the drug.
Maybe—if the cravings are subdued—
there's a chance she won't be crazy
till she dies. Still, I wonder why
a heroin addict who graduates
to methadone would ever leave
this dead end street. Methadone, like heroin
kills ambition, providing somnolence
without the bliss—the withdrawal's even worse.
It won't emaciate or get her locked up
by the cops, only make her fat and rot

her teeth. Invented by the same company
that created Zyclon B—
the chemical in Nazi gas chambers
that put everyone to sleep.

Higher Caliber Addict

I remember emerging from the Green Line T-stop
nearly bumping into her. I wasn't paying attention
to the street, focused inward on my daughter's fate,
asking why, begging please.

We were at the beginning, hopeful
that a Harvard-run program based on the science
of addiction would teach us how to help her
climb up from the Underneath.

We were walking to our weekly group
for parents of the fallen. I remember
it was May, the contrast between
the cherry blossoms on High Street
and the bird's nest of the old lady's
clumped, brackish hair.
She had parked her cart near a Greek column
at Government Center and was rummaging
through its skunky layers of survival-supporting junk.
I looked away with a shudder,
thinking this could be my daughter
in years to come—a limbo-dweller.

Five years later, she lives
in a dusty walk-up three blocks down,
saved by her inheritance—the pennies Grandpa accrued
on the humid factory floor—
wisely invested by Grandma, who could see beyond
the Camps and the south Bronx.
It's yours now honey, this small pot of money
to pay the cost of the roof over your head, the bed,
and your beloved TV. You can leave
each morning to swallow your liquid methadone,
lock the door and know you have a place to come home to.
You can be a higher caliber addict.

We didn't take the tough love road for long—
Motherlove won out. What my mother taught—
be kind to everyone you meet,
put a carton of milk on the table

of the needy, look straight
into reality's cold, dark eye—
and—at all costs, if you can help it—
don't let your family die.

Forty Acres & A Mule

This slave refuses her own plot of earth.
The rich brown soil lies fallow at her feet.

With care, it would support long stalks
Of yellow corn, fat green zucchinis.

But she's indifferent to what grows—
Except the poppy seed.

Oh the food she once cooked!
The pink salmon in creamy mango sauce

Seared meats and mushrooms simmered
In butter and wine, the regal meals she served

On a table set with fine china, crystal goblets,
Silver polished to a shine.

Now she eats fruit loops from a plastic bowl.

In the small shack she inhabits, she sits
In the dark, under the spell of the Master

Who tells her over and over:
You have no place in this world.

Detach With Love

What will survive of us is love
Philip Larkin

I no longer wake up on fire
My body does not ring
With the alarm of you

My clock is not set to spring
Into fruitless action. Not you
But the papers on my desk, spilling over

In haphazard piles, beckon me to rise,
Pour the chamomile tea.
A listlessness long banished

Returns, something akin to peace.
The first question I asked
Long ago at the first meeting

In a crusty room packed with mothers—
How does a mother detach
With love?

Had no answer I can remember.
Perhaps it's fatigue. The body stops fighting.
The war recedes.

The mammalian instinct to protect—
A worn machine—no longer turns over,
Sputters like an old lawnmower.

Will new shoots rise like grass
Between the cracks of cement
In a tree-less neighborhood?

In any case, there's always the sky.
When you come to my door,
The door is barred. From the porch

I throw down a pack of Newports

And a rolled-up ten-dollar bill.
I wish you well. I wish you well.

Love That Won't Let Up

It would be easy to sink
into the softness and be held up
by the weight of water, until the currents brought me
to the solid bottom, where nothing more
could break me. But we are fastened
to time's wheel, bound and chastened
by love that won't let up

Too Late

one day I fear you
won't wake up
and it will be too late
for you not to take
clonidine with promethazine
on top of klonopin
and methadone
too late to forgo
the cocktail
you've concocted
to resemble the ineffable
high of heroin
too late to make promises
you can't keep
to steep yourself in memories
of lost friends lost jobs
lost fun you had
when you had fun

one day I fear
I will bury you, my hair
will turn white
overnight as in a cheap
horror story and it will be
too late to check up on you
to see if
you're still breathing
and I will cry tears
dry tears
that vanish as they fall

Numbers Don't Include Suspected Deaths

Ten months after...Deval Patrick declared a public health emergency,
State Police recorded 114 suspected opioid fatalities in December, nearly
double the 60 that were tallied in November...numbers don't include
suspected deaths in Boston, Worcester, and Springfield.
The Boston Globe, January 29, 2015

No one's in a rush to count dead junkies

Reports, like corpses, pile up for years
Updates on the stats appear
In the news with repeated lacunae

They didn't count the deaths of queers
At the start of the AIDS epidemic until
Straight men who didn't stick their dicks up

Anyone's ass, and even women
Who had no idea how
The *faggot cancer* could infect them

Died   with the same finality
How many
Before the accounting?

Junkies when will you claim your names?
When will you rise up
From the streets for your own Stonewall riots?

When will you act up
And spit in the eye of smooth-talking politicians?
When will you demonstrate, holding signs: *Neglect=Death*?

When will you convene
A conference with the head of the CDC? When
Wake up and scream *Why are you letting us die?*

When will medical examiners stop
Packing you into morgues, throwing you
Down the chute to nameless graves

With only shamed families to mourn you?
Unseen (un)marked, with dark
Tracks on your scarred sacred bodies

Uncounted

Found Poem

Facebook, March 20, 2016
with permission from Beverley Straneva, in honor of her son, Timothy

My 32-year old boy died from an overdose last night, alone
in a Florida hotel. Not sure how to plan for a funeral.

Or for the rest of our lives—
he was our only child.

He sent me several texts yesterday morning.
Here's an excerpt from one:

I am powerless over a compulsive behavior
i cannot control. ..i am sick

and seeking my medicine as hard as i can....
im a good person...i love,

i want to be honest, im creative, im grateful,
i was raised by saints,....

i want the -- on my tombstone
to mean something. ...i am crying

everyday to a god im trying to believe in
to give me strength to help me move on...

and i know that if i survive this
i will bring a message to others just like me...

that it gets better. .i just haven't been able to grip
something others have...so i keep trying. ...

and there is nothing
you could have done different. ...

Demeter Goes Down

For nine long days and nights, each the equivalent of a year
I've had nothing to eat but my wrath
Nothing to drink but my tears.

I've sacrificed my throne,
Begged the gods for your return—
Aphrodite of the golden arms, Artemis, who with her twin

Apollo, killed all twelve children of Niobe,
Athena, the favored offspring of our father Zeus—
Useless—all of them!

Not a one understands
There is nothing
So strong as a mother's heart.

Not the thunderbolts of Zeus. Not the phallus
Of that rapist, Poseidon. Not the seductions
Of Hades, or his pomegranate trickery.

They say you are wed
To the God of Death.
They say I can't follow you down.

But I'm already here, in your room—
Sole witness to the cold needle's plunge
Into your hungry vein.

Hoping my presence will disgorge
Those seeds you eat to erase
Your memory of home.

I'm ready to stay for as long as it takes.

Going On Vacation

I'm standing in the cosmetics aisle deciding between
Neutrogena Ultra-Gentle Soothing Cream and
Lumene Rejuvenating Instant Serum. I'm weighing the pros
and cons of the luxurious unguent, which costs twice as much
as the more pedestrian brand. I'm rationalizing
it might be cost effective to purchase a moisturizer
so deep-penetrating and concentrated with active ingredients
to firm the skin and replenish it with natural radiance
that my haggard mug, appreciating the favor,
would reward me with something akin to pleasure.

On the other side of my brain, in the same aisle
at CVS, I am deciding whether to give my daughter
money for cab fare while I'm not here to chauffeur her
to methadone Mecca where she bows each morning to the god
of opiate addiction. Suppose she oversleeps, misses morning dose
and ends up in another relapse? It's not my place to prevent this,
as I have been told, repeatedly, by myself and others,
and really, let's face it, putting money in an addict's pocket
is always tricky if you don't want to be—God help me—
an enabler. In the same vein, I'm deciding what advice,
if any, to give her (since she's asked, a rarity)
on the question of what's safer—
whether to shelter the two crack addicts
currently relapsing in her apartment, or throw them out?

These two worlds co-exist, the face cream
and the crackheads, side by side.
I decide to go for the high-end serum, to give her
fifty bucks. I advise her to show the addicts the street.
The automated cashier sings
Please be sure to remove your bags and take your receipt.
Walking to the car I make a mental list:
pack flip-flops walking shoes beach towel dental floss.
Drop by her apartment with the cash
hug her and say: *This is for your health
and safety. I pray that's what you use it for.*
I've paid for the face cream. I'm ready
to vacation in the Caribbean.

84

Junkie

you should see the way they look at me
like shit beneath their shoes
like what did they used to call the jews
before the holocaust? vermin
i walk into a store and they barely let me in
i swear they can smell my history
on my body they follow me
to catch me stealing
and my fucking doctors too
they treat me like a felon it's like they rip open
the stitches in my mending heart and leave me broken
i'm trying to be more than a *junkie*
but mom you've never seen anyone look down
at someone the way they look at me

Colby Pond

For this one moment all the harm
    is in the past. The open water, clear and calm,
surrounds and holds us.

The green hillside in our line of sight,
    the quivering aspen on the shore, the gentle light
all combine to produce a sense that time

Has slowed, and has nowhere to go.

Out here, she says, facing up
    into the sky, as we swim out,
side by side, a*nything is possible.*

I want to say: is that you, my green-eyed girl,
    peeking out from behind the cloud that eclipsed—
for all this time—the dome of sky?

I want to say: Welcome home.

Vermont Summer

I'm the only human on this hill.
Abandoned ski chalets stare out of empty eye sockets.

The silence invites me
To fast and pray in the sun, sit on the rock

In the grove, fall on my knees
In the dark, talk to the striated spider.

I tell myself this weariness will pass,
Ask the earth to heal my collapse,

Search the ground for unseen clues,
Feed on the food the trees provide,

Lean on the mountain, sustained.
I submit my soul to be purified.

The light glints off the half-moon blade
My skin strips off—I'm flayed.

Civilization peels off me,
Leaving the pink, sensitive skin

Exposed to the light. The year returns like a beggar
Asking for last rites.

I burn in the blue fire
Of my daughter's immolation.

I walk with the junkies shuffling
In green slippers at Whittier Pavilion.

In the dawn's post-surgical pallor,
Lit by the hospital lights—blinking red and white—

Broken bones break again—atrophic scars
Burst open—

The grass whispers its secrets—
The six-eyed moth flies up—

The shards reassemble.

Orb Weaver

You must be still to see her—
  Catch the sun as it glints off
The steel-soft silk of her starburst mandala

At the top of the world she's spun
  From her body, she sits—
Her bulbous rear as round and gray as a pincushion

She only seems to sleep, compressed.
  Looking down, she surveys my readiness,
Moves quickly across

The gossamer, with her pincers
  Plucks a wayward line and packs it
Tightly back in place

Her hairy red-striped legs
  Wave and weave, convey
An ancient telegraphic language

Grandmother Spider,
  I am no longer afraid of you—
Amazement replacing all that dread!

Teach me to listen. Teach me
  To see. Teach me to know.
Teach me to be.

Weave close the nest, she says.
  With all your strength, repair
The broken thread—

But if beyond repair, let it dissolve—
  The ruptured fabric will not shred—
A tear will not undo the web

Epidemic

The Commonwealth is losing men and women on its streets at a rate of 42 to 1, compared to what the state is losing in two wars overseas.
The Massachusetts Oxycontin and Heroin Commission, quoted in The Boston Globe Nov. 6, 2009

They keep on dying,
She tells me. *More*
And younger each year.

Four people she knows
On the methadone dole, overdosed
In Boston this past month alone.

The latest batch of smack
Is cut with fentanyl—
Ground into a powder that,

Mixed with heroin, provides
A deadly double-whammy
Kind of high.

You ought to know—
You've got your bona fides.
You speak with the grief

Of direct expertise.
You're still here and can feel
The epic proportions of the epidemic.

From the crowded country of the (Un)Dead—
You've returned—my recognizable girl—
Your tears for the world, unzipped heart—

The same one you had at the start—
Before feeling too much
Became too much to bear

at the edge of the known

the lines once so precise split

apart and everything opens

into a vast ocean of air

the outlines of shapes

no longer approximate

anything you can name

or turn out to be

something else again—

that sleeping cat on the bed

is a sack of dirty laundry

look a bear   no it's a man

with a grizzled beard

he's coming to kill you   oh

he's bending down in prayer

she's done for   dead as a doornail

wait   there's life in the pale girl yet

she resurrects

don't trust a thing

it's always changing

black and white exchange places

find an unseen ally

to teach you how to see

then forget

everything you ever knew

it never stops

being interesting

learn to live

without knowing a thing

Nothing Is Ever Lost

God is washing me in a cauldron of scalding tears—
    With a hand-held crescent blade
        She is scrubbing away

My attachments. Drop by drop
    I'm wrung out clean and white
        as a starched sheet

Stretched tight and pinned
    on a line. Soon I will shine
        like amethyst, formed by centuries

Of lava flow. Remaining impurities
    will stain me indigo.
        From time to time, I will die—

No matter! Time and space are instruments to navigate
    the boundless—Fly through the black hole
        to remember the future—

Shake out space like a beach blanket—
    billowing waves of blue galaxies
        in the expansive darkness—

Nothing is ever lost—only transmuted—
    like ice to water—water to vapor—
        invisible—lighter—than air—

Cosmic Mother

I was Mother in another world
  Where energy has no need

Of body. Where Mothers have power
  To create, *ex nihilo,*

New beings. I was Queen
  In another world, long-limbed,

Radiant. Queen among Queens, I agreed
  To come to Earth

To lie down in the locked room of the body
  On a bed of spikes

To see spirit in the wounds
  To feel each mother's suffering

Until it reveals itself as Light

Can A Poem Save A Life?

I have lived like thin smoke, rising
  from a bloody field.

I have stretched my stringy will
  through one more night.

Not to forsake my child. Not to capitulate.
  To save a life

Is to save the world, the Talmud says.
  Can a poem save a life?

Shall I write new blood into dead words?
  Shall I peel back my sleeve?

Will the whisper of hope seep in-
  to the cordoned room

Of my loneliness? Shall I rise
  to one more morning?

Acknowledgments

I gratefully acknowledge the journals in which versions of the following poems originally appeared:
In Her Room; she's already gone   *Off the Coast*
Let's Talk About Addiction; Can a Poem Save a Life?   *The Healing Muse*

***

I am indebted to the many people—family, friends, poets, healers, writers, spirits, and members of the addiction/recovery community—who made this book possible by supporting my life with their presence, reading and responding to the work, and encouraging and making me a better poet.

My gratitude to the spirits who accompany and sustain me, for waking me up from my dreams with liminal broadcasts of first lines and whole poems. Without you, this book would not exist.

To Anna Gottlieb, for your generosity, and courage in reading these poems, offering your wise feedback, and giving them your blessing. For your kind heart and brave persistence in recovery. For returning to us.

To Roger Gottlieb, soul-mate and fellow soldier, thank you for sharing the foxhole and holding me up, time and time again. For listening to repeated readings of the poems through various incarnations and offering your kind and critical responses. For tolerating my obsessions and ruminations. For all this and more, I owe you my sanity (such as it is).

To Joanne Peterson, for sponsoring readings of these poems in thirteen towns in Massachusetts through your life-saving organization, Learn to Cope. And to the Learn to Cope families, who suffer daily with the epidemic and keep up their courage for the sake of their loved ones, thank you for your tears.   John F. Kelly, whose work in the field of addiction medicine and treatment has helped so many in recovery and contributed to de-stigmatizing addicts and their families, for your quick reading of the manuscript and readiness to lend your support to the poetry as a way to be of service to those who suffer with addiction in the family.

To Deena Metzger, for helping me take the poems out of hiding, for your close read-through of the early collection, and for offering asylum to my daughter and me. Kathleen Spivak, for your sharp eye and ear, for encouraging, scolding, and helping me create, from a pile of poems, a book. The 2015 Mass Poetry Festival, for hosting *The Poetry of Loss* and the opportunity to publically debut the poems. Joan Houlihan, Martha Rhodes and the Colrain Poetry Manuscript Conference, for your critical help with clarifying my poetic intentions and going forth as a poet. Barbara Helfgott Hyett, for calling these words "elegant poems about an inelegant subject," and for your helpful edit. Kathi Aguero, for your enthusiastic reading of the manuscript, astute suggestions, encouragement, and friendship. Julia Morris Paul, sister poet and mother-in-arms, for inviting me to do a solo reading for the 2015 Riverwood Poetry Series and understanding the importance of this subject in your forum *Something to Say: Poets and Conversations on Topics that Challenge,* and for your own extraordinary poetry from the addict's mother's perspective. Sheryl St. Germain, for reading and blessing the manuscript and our warm correspondence on the subject of creating and publishing art from the radical uncertainty and grief of loving someone who will not necessarily recover. Thank you for the brave, genuine, and beautiful poetry and prose you've written as the mother of a son lost to addiction.

To Carol Hymowitz, for your early encouragement for the first, tentative poems, your steadfast support for the larger project, and for the blessing of your friendship all these years. Harriet Lerner, for reading and supporting an early version of the work, for always being in my corner with compassion, understanding, sound advice, and a ready blurb. Phyllis Chesler, for championing these poems and suggesting they need to be read aloud on stage, for your help in trying to make it happen, and for your brilliant heart. Paula Caplan, for your quick reading and generous support in putting together a proposal for filming a one-woman show of the poetry. Anne Mackin, for your kind readings of some of these poems, and for our rejuvenating walks and talks.

To Harold Greenspan, for sound medical advice when we needed it and your good heart. Donna Semel, Scott Semel and John Sanbonmatsu for your unconditional friendship. Shannon Olin, for your gift as a holistic physical therapist, which, combined with your exquisite listening ear, kept me going, body and soul. Betsy Bergstrom for journeying on behalf of lost souls. Rachmiel Langer, wise Jewish shaman, for helping me see the brightest light in the darkest dark. Martha Kane, Jasen Boyle, Maureen Mcglame, and Mary McCusker for helping us survive the early days and years in the maelstrom.

To Aidla and Jacob Greenspan—may your memory be a blessing—for demonstrating that it is possible to survive the abyss and keep an open heart.

Finally, to Atmosphere Press for the perfect union of publishing professionalism and human connection. Nick Courtright, for your enthusiasm to publish this book and your diligent creative work on the project, including the design of the beautiful cover. Kyle McCord, for giving each poem an astute, eagle-eyed reading and applying your brilliant heart and mind to the book, improving it overall while respecting my intentions as an author. You are an author's dream of an editor.

About Atmosphere Press

Atmosphere Press is an independent, full-service publisher for excellent books in all genres and for all audiences. Learn more about what we do at atmospherepress.com.

We encourage you to check out some of Atmosphere's latest releases, which are available at Amazon.com and via order from your local bookstore:

The Unordering of Days, poetry by Jessica Palmer

It's Not About You, poetry by Daniel Casey

A Dream of Wide Water, poetry by Sharon Whitehill

Radical Dances of the Ferocious Kind, poetry by Tina Tru

The Woods Hold Us, poetry by Makani Speier-Brito

My Cemetery Friends: A Garden of Encounters at Mount Saint Mary in Queens, New York, nonfiction and poetry by Vincent J. Tomeo

Report from the Sea of Moisture, poetry by Stuart Jay Silverman

The Enemy of Everything, poetry by Michael Jones

The Stargazers, poetry by James McKee

The Pretend Life, poetry by Michelle Brooks

Minnesota and Other Poems, poetry by Daniel N. Nelson

About the Author

Miriam Greenspan, M.Ed., LMHC, is an internationally renowned psychotherapist, author, speaker, poet, and workshop leader, honored as a "feminist foremother" in psychology. Her pioneering book, *A New Approach to Women & Therapy,* helped define the field of feminist therapy. *Healing Through the Dark Emotions: the Wisdom of Grief, Fear, and Despair,* a Boston Globe bestseller, won the 2004 gold Nautilus Book Award in self-help/psychology for "books that make a contribution to conscious living and positive social change." It has been praised by Brene Brown, Harriet Lerner, Harold Kushner, Barbara Brown Taylor, and Dr. Christiane Northrup, among other cultural luminaries. Miriam's work has appeared in numerous anthologies and magazines, including The Sun, Huffington Post, Psychology Today, Spirituality & Health, Shambhala Sun, Ms., Psychotherapy Networker, and the Los Angeles Review of Books.

The Heroin Addict's Mother is her first book of poetry.

She can be reached at: www.miriamgreenspan.com